- A CARTOON NETWORK ORIGINAL -

D1500360

THE FAR-FROM-COMPLETE

COMPENDIUM

of

MAGISWORDS

by Brandon T. Snider

CARTOON
NETWORK
B O O K S

An Imprint of Penguin Random House

CARTOON NETWORK BOOKS
Penguin Young Readers Group
An Imprint of Penguin Random House LLC

MIGHTY MAGISWORDS, CARTOON NETWORK, the logos, and all related characters and elements are trademarks of and © Cartoon Network. (s18). All rights reserved. Published in 2018 by Cartoon Network Books, an imprint of Penguin Random House LLC, 345 Hudson Street, New York, New York 10014. Manufactured in China.

ISBN 9781101996171   10 9 8 7 6 5 4 3 2 1

Warriors for Hire are here!
It's the name and career!
Sleuthing siblings who quest!
Which is what they do best!
They have special tools!
For which they are fools!
These guys lose their mind,
when they collect or find the
Mighty Magi . . .

 swords.

Mighty Magiswords!!!!!

Greetings, weary traveler. My name is PROHYAS WARRIOR. My twin sister and I are WARRIORS FOR HIRE. We'll fight to the end if you ask nicely. Got a Magisword? Tell us where to go and we'll be there. If you're willing to pay the low price of fifty gems, we'll go wherever you want us to go and do whatever you want us to do.

I wouldn't go THAT far, Prohyas. We do have standards.

At WARRIORS FOR HIRE, where your issue is our mission! And now a little bit about me . . .

Favorite Animal: The dolphin (for reasons you'll understand very soon).

Favorite Pastime: Searching for Magiswords and finding Magiswords and using Magiswords.

Hidden Talent: I'm *really* good at playing the accordion.

Fun Fact: My hair is much silkier than Vambre's.

I am VAMBRE WARRIOR! I, too, share my twin brother's thirst for adventure. I've forged a courageous spirit for myself and won't back down from a fight. Especially if some naughty wastrel tries to challenge my family. Let's see, what else can I say?

Favorite Thing: Magiswords.

Least Favorite Thing:
I despise bullies and bullying behaviors. I also dislike wearing pants and refuse to let my legs be constricted by the confines of fabric.

Secret Weakness:
Weakness? HA! I've none.

What about your fear of squirrels?

SQUIRRELS?! WHERE? GET THEM OFF! GET THEM OFF!

Welcome to Ralphio's House of Swords! This dusty little Magisword shop is tucked neatly away inside Mount Ma'all in our cozy Kingdom of Rhyboflaven. Ralphio provides us with the Magiswords we need to complete our missions.

For a price. If you've got the gems, I've got the Magiswords.

Name: Ralphio Sabreware.

Function: Small-business owner.

Fun Fact: Ralphio loves haggling with customers and cutting deals with anxious Magisword-loving Warriors for Hire.

He's also got supersecret maps that lead to new and crazy Magiswords just waiting to be found. I get tingly just thinking about them. Hey, Vambre, do you think we can finally get that Cuddle Puppy Magisword while we're here?

Prohyas, you're broke.

Super Teamwork Combos are when two (or more) Magiswords combine their powers to become one awesome, ultimate attack!

Fun Fact: A Super Teamwork Combo doesn't need two Magisword wielders to be performed, it simply requires two awesome Magiswords.

Here are some of our favorites:

Cheese Magisword + Excaliburger Magisword = BELLY BURSTER!

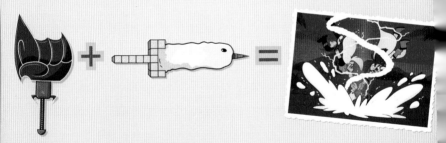

Ground Pound Magisword + Snowball Magisword = GRAVALANCHE!

Frog Missile Magisword + Wickersnapper Magisword = FROGTIED!

Abacus Magisword

Function: It does math.

Fun Fact: You need not lift a finger to move its beads from here to there. This Magisword does all the work for you.

Accordion Magisword

Function: It plays music . . .

Fun Fact: . . . because it's really just a regular run-of-the-mill accordion. Whenever someone is giving you a hard time and you want them to skedaddle, summon the Accordion Magisword and start playing. A few tunes later and they'll be running for the hills.

Acorn Arsenal Magisword

Function: Shoots large acorns.

Fun Fact: With light and water, acorns also can grow into trees. Science!

I use it to repel a renegade squirrel attack. UGH. I hate those nasty creatures.

WE KNOW.

All Ears Magisword

Function: It can hear things . . .

Fun Fact: . . . through walls and across far distances.

So keep your trap shut! This one loves secrets, too, so don't go blabbing any big ones when it's nearby. Don't talk about your sister's annoying habits, either, because *she will find out*. The fallout won't be pretty.

Anvil Magisword

Function: Shoots anvils.

Fun Fact: Anvils are heavy and it does NOT feel good when you're hit by them.

Attractive Voice Magisword

Function: Emits the sound of a *very* attractive voice.

Fun Fact: It says what it wants, when it wants, okay?

> Look at you, Prohyas. So strong. So smart. How about we find a nice place where we can be alone, huh?

Auto Style Magisword

Function: Styles hair of all types.

Fun Fact: This Magisword loves a challenge but, let's get real, if you're not conditioning properly then you're simply wasting its time.

> Trust me when I tell you, this thing works wonders. When I can't manage my mane, I fire up this bad boy (or is it bad *girl*?) and it does its thing. A lot of people think I'm wearing a wig, and I have to tell them THIS IS MY HAIR!

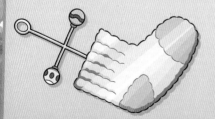

> Yes, but do you have to shout it in their faces?

Baby Booty Magisword

Function: Shoots baby booties of varying sizes.

Fun Fact: BOOTIES ARE TINY BABY SOCKS. THIS MAGISWORD DOES NOT SHOOT ANYTHING OTHER THAN TINY BABY SOCKS.

Bacon Magisword

Function: Shoots strips of crispy bacon.

Fun Fact: Bacon is considered delicious by many people.

Bag of Snakes Magisword

Function: Shoots burlap sacks filled with snakes.

Fun Fact: Snakes are frightful, slithering creatures that hiss and curl themselves around their enemies. Burlap sacks are a lot less dangerous. You can even use them as masks! On second thought, that's a bone-chilling sight. Just use them as burlap sacks and everything will be fine.

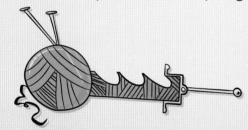

Ball of Yarn Magisword

Function: Can cover any object in yarn or make any object out of yarn.

Fun Fact: Yarn can also be used to make sweaters. Sweaters make great gifts.

Keep your granny busy for hours! Or anyone that loves yarn, really.

Ballpoint Magisword

Function: It's a pen. It writes.

Fun Fact: Its ink is permanent and comes in any color imaginable.

> I'm using this Magisword to write my memoir—*Tales of a Warrior for Hire*. If you know of an exemplary publisher who specializes in tantalizing tales of suspense and intrigue, do get in touch.

Banana Peel Magisword

Function: Shoots banana peels.

Fun Fact: Slipping on a banana peel is one of the greatest comedic devices of all time. Look it up.

Basketball Magisword

Function: Makes basketballs.

Fun Fact: The basketballs that this Magisword creates poof away magically once they've swooshed through a basket.

> I was wondering where they went!

Beehive Magisword

Function: Makes honey, honeycomb, beehives, and bees.

Fun Fact: Bees are very important to the environment in which they live. They can also sting you. It's not pleasant.

> SWEET. I meant about the honey, not the stinging.

Beginner Shield Magisword

Function: Acts as a very weak shield.

Fun Fact: This Magisword is easily broken and only good for one block before it breaks. It's a good thing they're cheap and plentiful!

Big Bad Boot Magisword

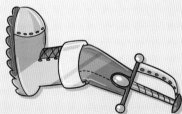

Function: Produces boots.

Fun Fact: This Big Bad Boot was made for busting down doors, knocking over sand castles, and kicking all sorts of stuff.

> What about bad guy rear ends?

> Indeed.

Birdcall Magisword

Function: Can replicate birdcalls that summon local birds to the area.

Fun Fact: This Magisword is best used sparingly because the last thing you need are hundreds of chirpy little birds following you wherever you go.

Bite Beast Magisword

Function: Creates strange little creatures that love to bite things.

Fun Fact: It hurts to get bitten by a Bite Beast!

Bling Bling Magisword

Function: Bedazzles things.

Fun Fact: Once an item has been bedazzled with the finest bling, its chances of being resold increase considerably.

Some might consider an item covered in shiny jewels to be gaudy and unappealing.

Do you?

No comment.

Blow Dryer Magisword

Function: Uses hot air to repel objects.

Fun Fact: Can also turn a soggy drain hair monster into a dried-up pile of crusty hair.

If you should find a ne'er-do-well trying to sneak up on you, simply summon the Blow Dryer Magisword and use one of its mighty GUSTS to send them away from your personage. It is also great for drying your hair.

Body Poppin' Magisword

Function: Makes people dance in the funkiest way you've ever seen. YA HEARD!

Fun Fact: Dancing is a great way to let your soul feel free! It's also a chance for your friends to find out if you have rhythm and coordination.

Bok Choy Magisword

Function: Produces bok choy.

Fun Fact: Bok choy is a vegetable that people either don't know anything about or despise.

Excuse me! Bok choy happens to be a hearty food that's filled with many nutrients and vitamins. Not everyone despises it. I quite enjoy a stalk from time to time.

You would.

Bonehead Magisword

Function: Shoots bones and bonemerangs.

Fun Fact: If the Magisword wielder concentrates, she (or he) may be able to shoot skulls and full skeleton bodies.

(Shhhh. I'm concentrating.)

Boomerang Magisword

Function: Shoots boomerangs that return no matter what.

Fun Fact: Boomerangs always return to their owner. Unless something terrible happens, like a giant gust of wind carries it far, far away or someone snatches the boomerang from the air and runs away with it. You might be thinking "What kind of ne'er-do-well would do such a thing?" Listen up! Rhyboflaven is filled with ne'er-do-wells and they will snatch a boomerang from the air and run away with it in a second. Trust.

We really should do something about this ne'er-do-well infestation.

Boulder Magisword

Function: Creates and shoots boulders.

Fun Fact: Prohyas and Vambre discovered it in a cave.

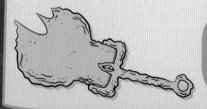

This large Magisword can be a bit tricky to wield. Perhaps one might find it useful to carry with them an over-the-shoulder Boulder Magisword holder?

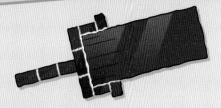

Brick Magisword

Function: Shoots bricks.

Fun Fact: Can also create brick walls and other brick-based formations.

Bronze Statue Magisword

Function: Turns anything into a heavy bronze statue.

Fun Fact: It can also turn heavy bronze statues back into whatever they were before. Neat, huh?

I wouldn't say *neat*.

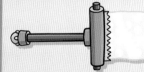

Bubble Pop Magisword

Function: Shoots plastic sheets of bubble-covered material.

Fun Fact: The Magisword wielder pops its bubbles to make loud noises. The bubbles then regenerate the next time the sword is unsheathed. This Magisword is known to annoy people to no end with all the *pop-pop-popping*.

It's also the perfect sword for shipping delicate items over long distances!

Bulldozer Magisword

Function: Bulldozes all kinds of stuff.

Fun Fact: Makes a solid snowplow but does NOT shape-change into a giant robot. Just to be clear.

Okay but does it dream of shape-changing into a giant robot?

Maybe. Sometimes. That's none of your business!

Bunch of Little Holes Magisword

Function: Can make a bunch of little holes in things, and can make a large thing into many tinier things.

Fun Fact: Also, great for blowing bubbles!

Butterfly Magisword

Function: Gives people butterfly wings.

Fun Fact: This Magisword builds a cocoon around its intended target, and when the cocoon falls away, the target is left with removable one-time-use butterfly wings.

Transformation is such an exciting prospect! To emerge from a warm swaddle, reborn anew! I've got shivers just thinking about it.

WINGS ARE JUST PLAIN COOL!

Cactus Magisword

Function: Shoots cactus balls.

Fun Fact: Cactus Magisword's jewel once belonged to Attackus, a giant cactus monster. It probably goes without saying, but be careful of the needles. *Yow!*

Cardboard Replica Magisword

Function: Creates flat cardboard replicas of things.

Fun Fact: Cardboard is very cheap and flimsy so, you know, don't expect to defend yourself with this Magisword. It's not really meant for that.

Carnivorous Plant Magisword

Function: Eats everything in its path.

Fun Fact: There's nothing fun about a plant that wants to eat you. NOTHING. What are you looking at? Get out of here before this thing gobbles you up! Do you even know what *carnivorous* means? Look it up, friend. If this Magisword sets its sights on you, you're done. And by *done*, that means it will eat you.

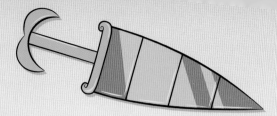

Carrot Magisword

Function: Can cut through any object.

Fun Fact: It can also create carrot slices of varying sizes.

This Magisword is our foe Hoppus's weapon of choice. He wields it well.

Thank you.

GAH! How did you get in here?

Check out *these* moves!

Not impressed.

Cat Tongue Magisword

Function: Licks stuff.

Fun Fact: Cat tongues are rough! Those things could lick the paint off a Hoversword.

Catnip Mouse Magisword

Function: Endlessly taunts cats and shoots catnip mice.

Fun Fact: Cats are very easy to taunt.

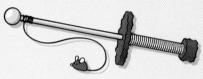

Oh no. Prohyas accidentally ate catnip.

GIVE ME THAT SWEET, SWEET CATNIP! I NEED IT!

Cayenne Pepper Magisword

Function: Creates super-spicy, fire-breath-inducing cayenne pepper.

Fun Fact: Stuffy nose? Fire a blast of cayenne pepper up your nostrils and it should clear right up. On second thought, don't do that. You'll *definitely* burn your nose and that would be terrible. Maybe take some medicine instead. Talk to your doctor first. This is a book about Magiswords, not a place for medical advice.

Fair enough!

Celery Magisword

Function: Shoots celery logs of varying sizes.

Fun Fact: It also makes things smell like celery.

Please respect Celery Magisword. If you don't, I'll use it to make your bedroom smell like celery. You don't want that.

Cement Truck Magisword

Function: Makes cement.

Fun Fact: If someone tells you that they want to give you a pair of cement shoes, run away from them and never look back!

Chain Saw Magisword

Function: Cuts through wood and other objects.

Fun Fact: NOT TO BE USED ON CAKES.

It can be a thrilling experience slicing through an obstruction of some sort, but be careful with this one. It's messy and imprecise and doesn't get along well with other Magiswords.

Cheese Magisword

Function: Fires cheese projectiles and creates objects made of cheese.

Fun Fact: People that hate cheese are the worst kind of people.

That's not true! That's just an *opinion*, not a fact.

Yeah, you're right. People that hate cheese are still *gouda* people.

Chillax Mist Magisword

Function: Releases a relaxing mist.

Fun Fact: Planning on attending Rhybofest, Rhyboflaven's number one (and only) music festival? Stop on by the Chillax Mist tent for a quick cool down!

Rhybofest used to be so cool and underground. Now it's just for sellouts.

Choo Choo Magisword

Function: Shoots trains and train paraphernalia.

Fun Fact: Trains are cool.

Did you hear about the thirsty train? It kept chugging no matter what.

Clapping Magisword

Function: It can clap, it can make others clap, and it can make its wielder clap.

Fun Fact: People love it when you clap for them. If the person wielding the Magisword claps, it may lead to them dropping the Magisword, which is embarrassing.

Confusing Alien Magisword

Function: It does whatever the heck it wants!

Fun Fact: This Magisword belongs to the living spaceships of Galacton and has exhibited the following powers: voice changing, shooting duckies (or summoning them), changing the colors of someone's clothing, creating a hole in the fabric of space-time, among many other mysterious abilities.

If I had a powerful Magisword like that, I'd make it scratch my back! That would be pretty awesome.

Cuddle Puppy Magisword

Function: Magically produces loads of live puppies.

Fun Fact: The puppies this Magisword creates will remain puppies forever and will never get any older or smarter. And if they get to be too much to handle? You can also use this Magisword to poof the puppies out of existence.

 NOOOOOOOOOOO! COME BACK, CUDDLE PUPPIES!!!

Cuppa Joe Magisword

Function: Produces coffee.

Fun Fact: "Cuppa Joe" is a nickname for coffee.

This makes perfect sense to me.

Dairy Product Magisword

Function: Shoots an assortment of dairy products. Moves include the Butter Blast, Ice-Cream Headache, and Cream-Cheese Please.

Fun Fact: It's shaped like a cow's udder!

At first I wasn't into this one but then Vambre told me about all its amazing abilities and I changed my mind. You could say she really *buttered* me up.

Dancing Bear Magisword

Function: Makes bears dance.

Fun Fact: There's a rumor that this Magisword can also *create* dancing bears.

Pshaw! Call me when there's a SINGING Bear Magisword. That's what I really want to see.

Give it time.

Darlin' Narwhal Magisword

Function: Creates cutesy little hearts.

Fun Fact: Narwhals are exactly like whales except they have a giant tusk sticking out of their head. Whales don't produce cutesy hearts from any part of their body, either. So maybe they're not so alike after all.

Dino Claw Magisword

Function: Grabs things.

Fun Fact: This Magisword belongs to King Rexxtopher.

 Why are there so many Magiswords that revolve around grabbing things? It doesn't make sense. We don't need all these grabby schmabby claws and stuff. Yes, it's a Dino Claw and dinosaurs are cool, but c'mon!

 You're just mad because it belongs to King Rexxtopher and not you.

 HA! That's just . . .

 Yeah, you're right. LOOK HOW COOL IT IS!

Dirt Magisword

Function: Makes dirt.

Fun Fact: Dirt is extremely dirty.

Diving Suit Magisword

Function: Shoots diving suits.

Fun Fact: Dream big, because this Magisword can create any kind of diving suit you can think of! All you have to do is concentrate.

Concentrating is hard.

Hey, look over there!

What was I saying?

Dolphin Magisword

Function: Shoots powerful blasts of water known as Dolphin Water. It also makes dolphin sounds.

Fun Fact: It must be fed three times a day and can also be used for quick underwater travel.

My baby! Who's a good Dolphin Magisword? It's YOU. Yes, it is. Yes, it is!

Squeak!

Aw, that's my girl. Your pips are music to my ears. Dolphin Magisword is one of my besties and the first Magisword I ever owned (thanks, Mom!). We've been through a lot together. Good times.

Droopy Clothes Magisword

Function: Shoots a liquid that makes clothes droop.

Fun Fact: Water is also a liquid that makes clothes droop.

So why not just throw water on someone?

That's no fun!

Dummystein Magisword

Function: Possesses the ability to steal someone's voice, like a ventriloquist dummy.

Fun Fact: Dummystein's jokes are not just terrible, they're the worst jokes you've ever heard in your life. Most people would rather hear two cats fighting in a room full of cymbals than listen to two minutes of Dummystein's act.

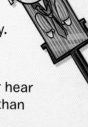

Electric Eel Magisword

Function: Fires an eel that bites down to release an electric charge.

Fun Fact: This Magisword can also be used like a whip. *OooOooO!*

I'm shocked to see Electric Eel Magisword here! SHOCKED.

Enough with your silly puns, brother.

Electric Guitar Magisword

Function: Produces sweet licks and powerful power chords.

Fun Fact: Playing the guitar may impress your friends, but your neighbors would love it if you could take up a different hobby. Sewing, perhaps?

Electric Razor Magisword

Function: It shaves things.

Fun Fact: Mustaches better beware!

The Electric Razor Magisword allows me to give my facial hair shape and form. With the flick of a wrist I'm able to create sideburns worthy of a true Warrior.

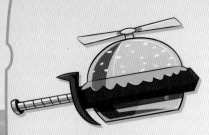

Excaliburger Magisword

Function: Shoots a nonstop stream of propeller burgers.

Fun Fact: Can carry the weight of a person.

Having an Excaliburger Magisword is like having your own personal helicopter. A big burger with a propeller that fires other tiny burgers with propellers? Now that, dear brother, is a weapon.

Excavator Magisword

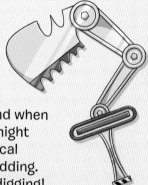

Function: Digs trenches.

Fun Fact: You never know what you'll find when you start digging into the ground. You might find an ancient alien species or a mystical staircase to another dimension. Just kidding. You'll find dirt. Plain ol' dirt. Now start digging!

Exploding Bubble Magisword

Function: Creates bubbles that explode.

Fun Fact: Prohyas and Vambre also use bubbles for transportation.

Hands off this one, brother! Exploding Bubble Magisword is all mine. I enjoy using Exploding Bubble Magisword to trap naughty evildoers. Of course, they don't enjoy it, but their feelings don't concern me.

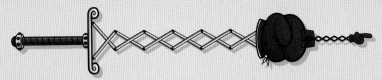

Extendo Flick Magisword

Function: Bops targets with its extendable boxing glove.

Fun Fact: This Magisword also contains a compartment with a smaller, flicking hand.

Fencing Magisword

Function: Creates any kind of fence imaginable.

Fun Fact: Yes, on the outside, it looks as if this Magisword only produces one kind of fence. Don't be fooled! Open your mind and let Fencing Magisword inside. Only then will you be able to create the FENCE OF YOUR DREAMS.

Fight Wig Magisword

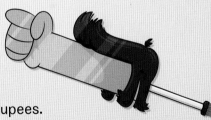

Function: Produces fighting toupees.

Fun Fact: Toupee fighting is illegal in many places.

This is the most disgraceful thing I've ever seen! These poor wigs just want to be loved. They simply want to be cared for and appreciated by their hairless owners. To pit them against one another is cruel and unusual and I am against it!

Fireworks Magisword

Function: Shoots fireworks.

Fun Fact: Fireworks are inherently fun and that's a fact!

They're also dangerous, so please use caution while wielding this Magisword!

Yes, use caution. And have fun!

Fish Head Magisword

Function: Extends to bop people on the head.

Fun Fact: It's a fish head on a stick. What's not to love?

THE STENCH! I CAN'T BEAR IT!

It's a fish head. It's not supposed to smell like roses.

Fish Stick Magisword

Function: Turns its target into a fish stick.

Fun Fact: The key to making the perfect fish stick is using the right amount of breading. You want to make sure it comes out a nice, golden brown.

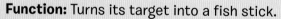

I should write this down.

Flashlight Magisword

Function: Shines light on things.

Fun Fact: It's just like a regular-size flashlight but bigger. Isn't that clever?

Flour Power Magisword

Function: Creates and shoots flour and flowers.

Fun Fact: Flour can be used to bake brownies, cookies, cupcakes, strudel, biscotti, and other delicious things. Flowers are cool, too, but you can't really eat them.

> Should you find yourself up against a foul enemy, consider giving them a flower. Don't shoot it at them! A peaceful solution must always be considered. Simply because one has the ability to shoot a flower, doesn't mean one should. 'Tis the secret to Flour Power.

Flyswatter Magisword

Function: Swats stuff.

Fun Fact: Not only is this Magisword perfect for swatting a pesky fly or two, it can also grow larger to swat enormous mutant flies. It can also be used as a spatula, but make sure you clean it first before you go flippin' flapjacks.

Foam Finger Magisword

Function: Creates celebratory foam fingers of various shapes and sizes.

Fun Fact: DO NOT USE THIS MAGISWORD TO PICK YOUR NOSE.

Gross. Who'd do something like that?

Don't look at me. I have petite nostrils.

Footprint Magisword

Function: Detects hidden footprints.

Fun Fact: It's perfect for tracking people who are running from their past.

Fossil Magisword

Function: Turns things into fossils that are embedded in giant pieces of rock. The sword can also undo the fossilization.

Fun Fact: Fossils are the preserved remnants of animals, plants, and other organisms from the distant past.

BO-RING!

FOSSILS ARE NOT BORING! YOU'RE BORING!

Fresh Squeeze Lemon Magisword

Function: Makes lemonade, limeade, and any assorted ade you can imagine.

Fun Fact: Ades taste GOOD.

Let's make MOLLUSKADE! Mmmmmmmmm.

No.

Frog Missile Magisword

Function: Fires froglike missiles that explode into live frogs when they hit their target.

Fun Fact: It shoots in ALL directions.

Fuzzy Wuzzy Magisword

Function: Makes things furry and fuzzy.

Fun Fact: When using this Magisword on an assailant, resist the urge to cuddle them once they've been covered in soft, furry fuzz. Just because they're cuddle-worthy doesn't mean they aren't still trying to destroy you.

Thanks for the tip!

Giant Egg Magisword

Function: Shoots giant chicken eggs.

Fun Fact: This Magisword can shoot eggs that have been prepared in a variety of ways: scrambled, sunny-side up, poached, and more. It can also shoot the eggs of creatures other than chickens.

Yikes.

Glamour Gown Magisword

Function: Clothes its target in a fabulous gown.

Fun Fact: Not everyone likes being clothed in a fabulous gown. That's part of the fun!

Glo-Stick Magisword

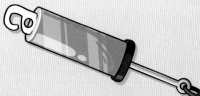

Function: Makes glow sticks.

Fun Fact: Your friend who goes out dancing all the time is going to ask you to make a bunch of glow sticks once they find out you own this. Just be aware of that.

Golden Broomstick Magisword

Function: Flies and is great for sweeping.

Fun Fact: This luxury broom is a very rare Magisword used by Witchy Simone to fly across Rhyboflaven.

Golden Curls Magisword

Function: Turns someone's hair into a pile of golden curls.

Fun Fact: Having curls is NOT the same as having a perm.

I learned that the hard way.

Grabby Giraffe Magisword

Function: Grabs things with its giraffe mouth.

Fun Fact: You may want this Magisword to speak to you like a stuffy old giraffe but, remember, it doesn't talk. It only grabs.

Ground Pound Magisword

Function: Causes earthquakes when striking the ground.

Fun Fact: Vambre recovered it after defeating the Underground Handbeast. Be very careful when using such a powerful Magisword. It packs quite a wallop in battle. Should not be used frivolously.

Gummy Sticky Hand Magisword

Function: Uses a gummy sticky hand to grab things.

Fun Fact: It's unable to attach itself to snow.

Sure, I can use Gummy Sticky Hand to swing around or smack a bad guy, but that's not the best part. The real magic happens when I'm lying on the couch and my Slug Burger is on the table. With the flick of my wrist, Gummy Sticky Hand Magisword brings it right to me. Am I just lazy? Maybe, but Gummy Sticky Hand Magisword doesn't judge.

Homing Device Magisword

Function: Fires a homing device that can be traced.

Fun Fact: Only comes with one tracer, so use it wisely.

Hook Magisword

Function: Does hook stuff. Also extends.

Fun Fact: The hook will ALWAYS bring you back.

Hot Oil Magisword

Function: Produces hot oil.

Fun Fact: This Magisword is great to use when your hair is dry and needs a little nourishment. Be careful when using. *HOT* means *HOT*.

I also learned *that* the hard way.

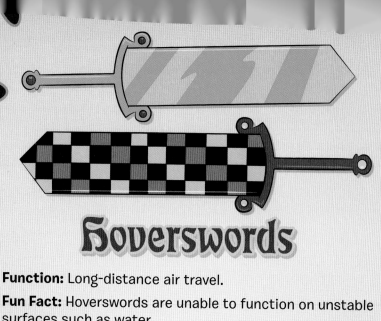

Hoverswords

Function: Long-distance air travel.

Fun Fact: Hoverswords are unable to function on unstable surfaces such as water.

Like our Hoversword designs? We made them ourselves.

I'm known for my artistic flair.

Hypno Magisword

Function: Hypnotizes its owner.

Fun Fact: It's unable to hypnotize anyone *other* than its owner. What a rub!

Instant Wrap Magisword

Function: Packages and decorates things.

Fun Fact: Is it your brother's birthday but you don't have anything to wrap his gift with? Don't worry! Fire up this Magisword and you're saved! Not only that but you can use it to wallpaper your downstairs bathroom.

 Thank heavens! I don't know what I would do without such an inventive device!

Jackhammer Magisword

Function: Breaks up rock and other sturdy materials.

Fun Fact: Jackhammers are incredibly loud.

 Rock 'n' roll!

Kite Magisword

Function: Makes kites that can fly on their own.

Fun Fact: Kites filled with passion and vigor can fly into space. Dream big, little kites!

Laser Pointer Magisword

Function: Creates a red beam of light that attracts cats of all kinds.

Fun Fact: In addition to attracting *classic* felines, this Magisword also attracts humanoid cats typically known as Cat People.

Legendary Hyperspace Magisword

Function: Has the power to transport the wielder to wherever it chooses.

Fun Fact: A first-time wielder always ends up in a random place. It's currently unknown whether a skilled wielder can determine where they're transported.

Ooooooo! What a curious mystery. Prohyas, if you could be transported anywhere imaginable, where would you go?

That's easy. SLUG BURGER! Great burgers, great service. I love it there!

Utterly predictable.

Thanks!

Legendary Knowledge Magisword

Function: It absorbs the knowledge of whomever the wielder points it toward.

Fun Fact: This Magisword is said to hold all the knowledge throughout Adventure Academy's long history. That's a lot of knowledge.

Absorb my knowledge! Absorb my knowledge!

No, thank you.

Levitation Magisword

Function: Moves people and objects around as the wielder wills.

Fun Fact: And it can be used hands-free!

Little Blue Bomb Magisword

Function: Shoots little blue bombs.

Fun Fact: Does NOT shoot big red bombs.

Be very cautious when using this Magisword. One *wouldn't* want to shoot a little blue bomb on accident, *would one*?

I thought we weren't going to talk about "the incident."

Lobster Claw Magisword

Function: Grabs and holds things using a lobster claw.

Fun Fact: The claw can also function as pliers. The perfect Magisword for twisting the lids off difficult jars, or chopping produce. You can also add a dab of melted butter to create a delicious meal worthy of a king!

Looming Loom Magisword

Function: Makes fabric out of just about anything.

Fun Fact: It may look like a regular ol' loom; however, its wielder must remain wary. This Magisword is surrounded by a curious and foreboding aura.

What does that even mean?

It means BE CAREFUL.

Oh.

Magnet Magisword

Function: Shoots a powerful magnet beam that pulls metal toward it.

Fun Fact: The beam also attracts other Magiswords.

Magnifying Glass Magisword

Function: Magnifies objects.

Fun Fact: Giants and ogres LOVE this thing.

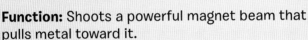

Mask Magisword

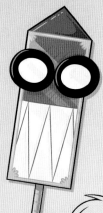

Function: Shoots masks onto people's faces.

Fun Fact: The mask's expression takes on the emotional state of the Magisword wielder. Whoever is wearing the mask then feels that emotion as well.

So if you're angry and shoot a mask at me then I turn angry, too?

Yes. Although, I'm generally in an upbeat mood so there isn't anything to worry about.

HA! Sure.

Meat Grinder Magisword

Function: Grinds things into sausage.

Fun Fact: Most people believe that meat is the only thing that can be ground into sausage. Not true! This Magisword will grind just about *anything* into beautiful little sausage links. Give it a go and see.

But then why call them sausages if they're made of other materials?

Mechanical Mole Magisword

Function: Digs through and gnaws on things.

Fun Fact: It looks exactly like a mole. If a mole was made of metal and attached to a magic sword, that is.

Mega-Drill Magisword

Function: Drills stuff. IN A MEGA WAY.

Fun Fact: It's good for burrowing and, you know, drilling.

Microphone Magisword

Function: Amplifies voice and sound like a microphone is known to do.

Fun Fact: People are generally terrified of speaking in public.

Microphone Magisword is great for shouting orders, like when I'm at Slug Burger and Witchy Simone is droning on and on about how she wants to "go back to school" because "learning is cool." Then I have to be all "CAN YOU PLEASE JUST GIVE ME MY SLUG BURGERS WITH EXTRA NEWT, LETTUCE, AND TOMATO. PLUS, A BELCH ZERO WITH LIGHT ICE?" I'm not about the small talk when my tummy is rumbling and needs to be fed.

Microwave Magisword

Function: Cooks stuff.

Fun Fact: It's not the most trustworthy Magisword and has been known to conk out while in the middle of heating up a tasty dish.

Tell me about it! How many times have I tried heating up a leftover Slug Burger only to find it's still cold in the middle?

A million times?

A million times!

Missing Sock Magisword

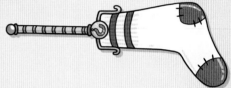

Function: Magically summons all nearby socks, which then stick to the summoner via static electricity.

Fun Fact: Socks come in pairs! Unless you're a three-legged beast and have your socks made special by a guy named Blurp who lives in a cave.

Monobrow Magisword

Function: Shoots an adhesive monobrow.

Fun Fact: Some cultures believe that beautiful, majestic monobrows should be shaved into two disgusting single brows.

Gross!

Which part?

All of it!

Monster Suit Magisword

Function: Dresses its target up in a cheap monster suit.

Fun Fact: People define the word *cheap* in different ways. Some think it means a level of affordability, while others believe it denotes a lowering of quality. Either way, monsters are cool and that's all that matters.

Mop Magisword

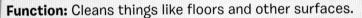

Function: Cleans things like floors and other surfaces.

Fun Fact: You can pretend Mop Magisword is a microphone and you're the lead singer in a band, rocking out in front of a whole stadium filled with fans. Or you can just use it to mop. It's up to you.

Get ready for some wet justice!

Mousetrap Magisword

Function: Makes mousetraps.

Fun Fact: The mousetraps created by this Magisword can be as difficult or complicated as its wielder desires. Life is about choices.

Mummy Magisword

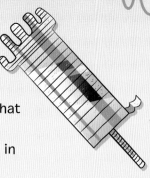

Function: Fires mummified bandages that can wrap an opponent entirely.

Fun Fact: Bandages do not break apart in water. Sorry.

Muscly Arm Magisword

Function: Makes someone's arm disproportionately larger and stronger.

Fun Fact: The effects are only temporary but the sight of seeing your arm veins grow to the size of licorice will be burned into your brain forever.

Nail Clipper Magisword

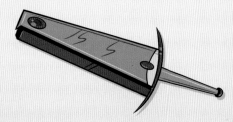

Function: It clips nails.

Fun Fact: Is there anything fun you can say about a nail clipper?

This Magisword is quite inferior, but does have its uses when the need arises in the form of a hangnail.

Needlessly Complicated Magisword

Function: Makes objects and situations way more complicated than they need to be.

Fun Fact: There's nothing fun about a needlessly complicated situation.

Ninjappearance Magisword

Function: Dresses its target in ninja-related apparel.

Fun Fact: Just because you're dressed like a ninja, doesn't mean you *are* a ninja. Remember that. Write it on your hand if you must. Never forget it.

Done.

Normcore Magisword

Function: Dresses its target in boring, unfashionable clothes.

Fun Fact: Should you get blasted with this Magisword, don't be surprised if people on the street ignore you. Life is meant to be lived with flair! Not a sensible jacket.

I agree wholeheartedly. That's why I like some style with my substance.

You call that style?

I beg your pardon?

What? Who said that? I didn't say anything. I'm just Fun Facts. Bye!

Oinkus Oinkus Magisword

Function: Releases a deafening squeal that can push things backwards.

Fun Fact: Vambre enjoys brushing this one. A LOT.

My piggy pal always protects me from evildoers and miscreants. Should a naughty brigand attempt to pilfer my gems, I simply aim Oinkus Oinkus and . . .

SQUEEEEEEEEEEEEEEEE!

Ointment Magisword

Function: Shoots ointment.

Fun Fact: The ointment released by this Magisword erases the effects of magic. But you've got to take the cap off first.

GAH! I always forget to do that!

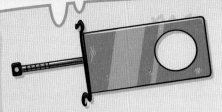

One Big Hole Magisword

Function: Makes a big hole in whatever nonliving thing its wielder wants to make a big hole in.

Fun Fact: One Big Hole Magisword and Bunch of Little Holes Magisword are brothers. One is jealous of the other and they argue sometimes when the other Magiswords are resting. But you can't tell anyone! It's a secret.

I never knew that!

Of course you didn't. You never read my Magisword fan fiction. Never!

Onion Magisword

Function: Smells like an onion and makes people cry.

Fun Fact: Smelling like an onion and making people cry are traits that Onion Magisword shares with Ralphio.

Hey! That's not true.

Oogly Googly Eyes Magisword

Function: Uses prehensile eyes to punch things.

Fun Fact: This Magisword's bizarre appearance tends to unnerve both its wielder and its intended target. It also has a serious effect on scaredy-cats.

Opposable Thumb Magisword

Function: Does whatever a giant thumb does.

Fun Fact: Opposable Thumb doesn't need a bunch of silly fingers holding it back. It's a big pink thumb! Nothing will stand in its way. Nothing!

What if it gets hit with a hammer or someone accidentally closes a door on it?

Well, then we've got a problem.

Pan Flute Magisword

Function: Makes its own kind of music.

Fun Fact: This Magisword produces a sound that will entice mice to follow its wielder. Who doesn't love the dulcet tones of a pan flute?

Well . . .

DON'T YOU ANSWER THAT!

Pancake Magisword

Function: Creates strong disc-like flapjacks that can be fired at an opponent. Think of them as floppy little Frisbees.

Fun Fact: Together with Waffle Magisword, it's part of a tasty breakfast.

Pandachute Magisword

Function: It's a parachute with a panda on it!

Fun Fact: So . . . much . . . cute . . . can't . . . handle . . . it.

What a lovable little parachute! It makes me want to jump out of a plane and into a big fluffy bed covered with snuggle muffins.

Paper Bag Magisword

Function: Makes paper bags.

Fun Fact: This Magisword can also make sentient paper bag puppets that sound curiously like sad lounge singers who've got a song in their heart and no place to stay for the night.

 Ouch!

You're tellin' me, kid. Don't forget to tip your paper bag, huh?

Parrot Scissors Magisword

Function: It's a pair of scissors and a parrot that repeats what it hears.

Fun Fact: DO NOT RUN WITH PARROT SCISSORS MAGISWORD OR SPILL ANY SECRETS WHILE IT'S IN YOUR GENERAL VICINITY.

 This is an annoying Magisword if ever there was one.

 This is an annoying Magisword if ever there was one.

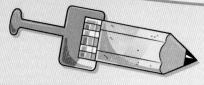

Pencil Magisword

Function: It writes.

Fun Fact: If you have trouble finding your pencil, don't forget, it's probably behind your ear. Lots of people forget they put it there. Or it might be at the bottom of the sea. Who knows? People are different.

Pencil Magisword is one of the most trustworthy weapons I own. It's always there when I need it the most. I'll be honest, it makes me feel like a real hero. I also use it to draw mustaches.

Pencil Sharpener Magisword

Function: Turns a piece of wood into a sharpened pencil.

Fun Fact: It sharpens anything you put in it! But let's not go crazy.

Perfume Magisword

Function: Makes things smell like perfume.

Fun Fact: Not everyone enjoys the smell of perfume. Some individuals find it particularly haunting.

I think perfume smells a bit like someone strangled a bouquet of beautiful flowers, soaked them in pungent liquid, and then left that liquid sitting in the hot sun for a week till it bubbled like a cauldron full of witches' brew.

Permanent Vacation Magisword

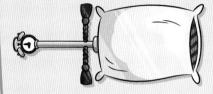

Function: Dresses the target in vacation-related clothing.

Fun Fact: When wearing vacation-related clothing, the target becomes overwhelmed by the desire to go on vacation.

Pillow Magisword

Function: Shoots pillows.

Fun Fact: This Magisword is very soft and comfortable, despite its cold, flat, metal frame. It's great for a mid-battle snooze or adventure-based nap.

There's no napping during adventures!

But what if my eyes get heavy and I need a little shut-eye?

WAIT TILL YOU GET HOME.

Pixel Magisword

Function: Transforms its target into flat digital pixels.

Fun Fact: A pixel is a small area of a digital display screen, one of many from which an image is comprised.

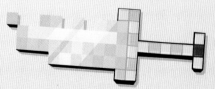

Hey! This Magisword makes everything look like an old video game. Cool.

What's a . . . video game?

Pizza Magisword

Function: Makes pizza.

Fun Fact: This Magisword can make cheesy, mouthwatering pizza at any temperature that the wielder finds appropriate.

Plunger Magisword

Function: Unclogs sinks and toilets.

Fun Fact: It can also stick to surfaces using suction! Isn't that cool?

Eh. Not really.

WELL, PLUMBERS THINK IT'S COOL AND THAT'S ALL THAT MATTERS.

Pogo Stick Magisword

Function: Hops up and down.

Fun Fact: The pogo stick was invented by Larry Pogo, a very tiny gentleman who had trouble reaching things on high shelves.

Even I know that Fun Fact isn't true.

Well, I guess you know everything, don't you?! Sorry. It's been a very long day.

Been there, pal.

Rad Rocket Magisword

Function: Uses rocket-power propulsion for air travel.

Fun Fact: It's VERY difficult to control.

You know how sometimes you'll be standing in front of a mountain with no way to get up to the top and you think to yourself, *Self, how the devil am I going to get up there?* Well, worry no more. Summon Rad Rocket Magisword and blast off high into the sky! You'll reach the top of that mountain in no time. Hopefully. It kind of has a mind of its own.

Radiator Magisword

Function: Makes things very hot, creates steam, and can shoot fire.

Fun Fact: It gets hotter the more that it's used. Check the settings—when it's red, that means it's ready to go ballistic.

Rain Cloud Magisword

Function: Creates clouds that produce rain.

Fun Fact: Not only can rain clouds be used for transportation but they also make great hiding places.

Rain clouds are perfect for when you need an on-the-go shower. Sometimes when I'm adventuring I can work up quite a stink.

Really? I hadn't noticed. I assumed that foul smell was a poor unfortunate forest creature that had eaten something troubling.

Rainbow Glasses Magisword

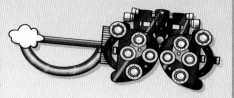

Function: Creates glasses through which bold color effects can be viewed.

Fun Fact: Not to be confused with Rose-Colored Glasses Magisword, which is not a real Magisword, merely an optimistic state of mind.

Retractable Ladder Magisword

Function: Extends for use as a ladder.

Fun Fact: This Magisword does not have an infinite reach; however, it can go very far, so that's something.

I like to use Retractable Ladder Magisword to reach things that are far away when I'm lying down on the couch. Comes in handy!

I prefer to use it as a classic ladder, traditionally used for reaching high spaces including bookshelves and cabinets.

Robo-Tank Magisword

Function: Shoots tiny tanks.

Fun Fact: These lovable itty-bitty little tankies will DESTROY EVERYTHING IN THEIR PATH BECAUSE THEY'RE STILL TANKS.

Rodeo Magisword

Function: Becomes flexible for use as a lasso.

Fun Fact: This Magisword can also summon bulls, clowns, and, strangely enough, barbecue sauce. Don't ask.

I don't need this Magisword to summon some barbecue sauce. All I need is the power of my own voice. Barbecue sauce! Oh, barbecue sauce! Where art thou, barbecue sauce?!

Oh dear. I think I see a clown riding a bull in the distance and it's headed this way.

Roundabout Magisword

Function: Changes the direction in which its intended target is headed.

Fun Fact: In life, sometimes we need a Magisword that taps us on the shoulder and says, "Hey. Hi. Maybe it's time to try something new?"

Pardon me, but I'm afraid this Magisword isn't all that deep.

Why can't you just let it have its moment?

Roundy Spinny Thing Magisword

Function: You know those roundy spinny things that make cats go insane? This is that, in sword form.

Fun Fact: It can also make things spin within a designated roundy area.

Rubber Spiky Magisword

Function: Shoots rubber spikes that grow back after release.

Fun Fact: Despite its frightening appearance, this Magisword isn't as dangerous as it might look. It's harmless and, honestly, quite fun under the right circumstances.

Which circumstances are those?

The kind where you can shoot a rubber spike at someone who asks too many questions.

I see.

Rubber Stamp Magisword

Function: Stamps an image on any surface.

Fun Fact: You're probably asking yourself, what's on this stamp? That's entirely up to the wielder. Feel like stamping a smiley face on the back of your hand? Go for it! Or maybe you want to stamp the words *HELP ME* on a slip of paper and then hand it to someone you meet in a Slug Burger? That's also an option.

Rump Roast Magisword

Function: Shoots slabs of nonspecific red meat.

Fun Fact: Nonspecific Red Meat is not the name of a band. But it should be.

Only if I can be the lead singer.

Rutabaga Magisword

Function: Makes rutabagas.

Fun Fact: Chop a rutabaga into thin slices, put them on an oiled baking sheet with a sprinkle of salt, then pop them in the oven and you've got tasty rutabaga chips.

Are we just doing recipes now?

I'm in! I'll make a stew.

Sea Salt Magisword

Function: Makes salt of varying sizes and shapes.

Fun Fact: Is the walkway to your headquarters covered in snow and ice? Use this Magisword to create salt crystals and watch the ice melt away in seconds.

It's more like minutes.

Depending on the size of the salt crystals, it could be more like hours.

THANKS. I GET IT. I WAS JUST TRYING TO HELP.

Who are you, anyway?

Selective Memory Magisword

Function: Erases whatever part of someone's memory the wielder wishes to erase.

Fun Fact: Ain't nothin' fun about this one.

 This Magisword is frightening indeed. Prohyas, can you imagine having your memory stolen?! The thought makes me shiver.

Who's to say our memories haven't been stolen already? We could have had a giant battle with an evil villain who used the Selective Memory Magisword on us but we'd never remember because he (or she) stole that memory and left us with nothing.

Oh dear.

Shark Blade Magisword

Function: Chomps through just about anything.

Fun Fact: It can also swim and breathe underwater. A threatening weapon if ever there was one.

Shuffle Magisword

Function: Changes the order of something.

Fun Fact: Don't do any important filing around this thing.

Sleeping Dragon Magisword

Function: Fires a beam that puts people and creatures to sleep.

Fun Fact: Prohyas and Vambre accidentally put themselves to sleep. It happens more than they'd like to admit.

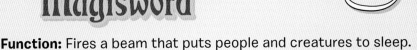

ZZZZZZZZZZZZZZZZZZZZZZZZZZZZZZZZ.

ZZZZZZZZZZZZZZZZZZZZZ.

Slime Magisword

Function: Shoots slime.

Fun Fact: It's super fun to watch someone get covered in ooey-gooey slime.

That's true! But when you're the one getting slimed, it's not so cool. Okay, maybe sometimes it is. Depends on the day. And the temperature of the slime.

Slingshot Magisword

Function: Slings things through the air.

Fun Fact: This Magisword varies in size and can be used to sling large objects.

It's perfect for slinging nachos into your friend's mouth.

Smelly Shoe Magisword

Function: SMELLS TERRIBLE.

Fun Fact: GET THAT THING OUT OF HERE!

Snowball Magisword

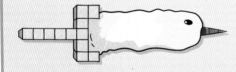

Function: Shoots snowballs and freezes things.

Fun Fact: Snow is very cold.

I've faced down many a surly behemoth in my time. When all hope seemed lost, I turned to Snowball Magisword for assistance. It's really quite lovely. It allows me to freeze my enemies quickly and efficiently. What more could a Warrior want in life?

Snow Cone Magisword

Function: Creates snow cones of varying flavors.

Fun Fact: This Magisword can also be used to make big, snowy avalanches.

> Mmmmmm. I think I want a grape-snow-cone avalanche.

> I shall try a rainbow of all the wonderful flavors!

> Can I change my order?

Soothing Brush Magisword

Function: Brushes stuff.

Fun Fact: This brush-shaped Magisword can calm down its intended target with a simple stroke, leaving them feeling refreshed and invigorated.

MUST BE NICE.

Spiderweb Magisword

Function: Shoots spiderwebs.

Fun Fact: The webs made by this Magisword also produce an onslaught of tiny spiders. Sweet dreams!

> To get this beauty we had to fight a giant spider in a castle.

> She covered us in her spider children. I could have done without that part.

Springtime Magisword

Function: Changes weather conditions within a small area.

Fun Fact: Bringing about weather shifts can cause new and exciting things to grow!

Spring is such a delightful time. Flowers bloom, butterflies emerge from their cocoons, and Prohyas washes his tunic for the first time in months. Truly magical!

Squeaky Nightstick Magisword

Function: Bops people on the head.

Fun Fact: This billy club may look threatening, but it's totally harmless. Unless you have a fear of billy clubs, then you're probably freaking out right now.

Sticky Note Magisword

Function: Creates sticky notes.

Fun Fact: The wielder of this Magisword needn't spend time doodling a message onto each sticky note. She (or he) must simply think of what they'd like it to say and POOF! The message appears. What will they think of next, am I right?

Cover an enemy in tiny little reminders!

Stirring Spoon Magisword

Function: Stirs things.

Fun Fact: This Magisword is perfect for the on-the-go cook. It stirs things quickly, evenly, and with aplomb. It's also nice because it gives your poor wrist a rest.

 That's awesome. Using Magiswords all day eats up a lot of energy. My wrist needs a rest. Does it rub feet, too?

NO.

Okay. Just checking.

Stuffed Animal Magisword

Function: Shoots stuffed animals.

Fun Fact: Is your brother feeling down? A stuffed animal might cheer him up!

 What a superb idea! Would you like that, Prohyas?

 I'd rather have more Magiswords. And more Slug Burgers. But thanks! It's the thought that counts.

Sun Face Magisword

Function: Glows, warms things, and shoots little sun faces.

Fun Fact: The sun is VERY hot. Do not touch the sun.

Super Shooting Star Magisword

Function: Shoots stars of varying sizes and shapes.

Fun Fact: It's sparkly.

This is one of my favorites! It gives me hopes. It fills my dreams. It makes me believe that I can reach beyond the heavens themselves and into the great unknown. WHAT? I can be deep sometimes.

Swish Navy Magisword

Function: Serves as a multipurpose travel device with over one hundred different uses.

Fun Fact: This Magisword comes from the strange world of Swisherland. *OoOoO!* Its true capabilities remain cloaked in mystery but it's been known to function as a hacksaw, trumpet, tentacle, knife, corkscrew, scissors, catcher's mitt, buzz saw, cuckoo, and kitty.

Tape Measure Magisword

Function: Slings an abnormally long measuring tape.

Fun Fact: Can also be used as a grappling hook.

Taunting Jester Magisword

Function: Annoys people.

Fun Fact: This loudmouth Magisword shouts orders at his unwilling targets and uses mind control to convince people to do his bidding. FUN fuels his cruelty. Good luck controlling this one. It's got a mind of its own.

> Awww, go blow it out your One Big Hole Magisword!

> Watch your tongue, vile creature!

Telescope Magisword

Function: Extends to become a powerful telescope.

Fun Fact: This Magisword, as powerful as it is, cannot see into our hearts.

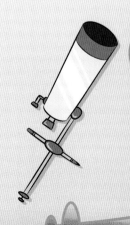

This Way Magisword

Function: Pulls its wielder in whatever direction the sword is facing.

Fun Fact: DON'T point this Magisword toward the sky. You don't want to know what happens.

Yes, I do!

Tickle Magisword

Function: Tickles people.

Fun Fact: Some people do not like to be tickled. At all. Not even as a joke. If you try to tickle them they'll swat your hand away and push you off your chair.

Toboggan Magisword

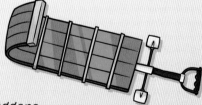

Function: Shoots toboggans.

Fun Fact: This Magisword can grow larger to become a completely usable toboggan.

Tomato Magisword

Function: Shoots tomatoes.

Fun Fact: Tomatoes are considered fruits not vegetables.

This was my very first Magisword. Do you remember, Prohyas? Mother gave it to me when I was a wee girl. So many wonderful memories of launching enormous squishy tomatoes toward my enemies.

Toothbrush Magisword

Function: Shoots toothbrushes.

Fun Fact: It also cleans teeth. GO FIGURE!

Trouser Magisword

Function: Makes pants. Any style. Any size.

Fun Fact: You must always put on pants before leaving your headquarters. Some Warriors for Hire have had to learn this lesson the hard way.

Umbrellaphant Magisword

Function: It's an umbrella and an elephant.

Fun Fact: Anything is possible in this topsy-turvy world. Even an Umbrellaphant.

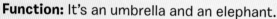

Underpants Magisword

Function: Makes underwear of varying sizes and shapes.

Fun Fact: This Magisword produces some of the stretchiest underpants in all Rhyboflaven. The kind that everyone is talking about.

Unravel Magisword

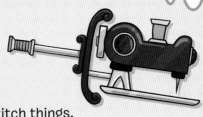

Function: Used to untie and unstitch things.

Fun Fact: Be careful what you unravel with this thing. Most people prefer their clothing remain intact!

Veg-A-Splode Magisword

Function: Shoots out exploding plant food.

Fun Fact: If your green thumb is lacking, you can use Veg-A-Splode Magisword to put some extra pep in your peppers.

And a bit of *care* in your carrots!

Wad of Gum Magisword

Function: Shoots wads of pink chewing gum.

Fun Fact: Gum is fun to chew! But don't swallow it. That's bad.

If the roof to your headquarters is falling apart, just launch a couple wads in its direction and it'll fix right up.

Waffle Magisword

Function: Shoots waffles.

Fun Fact: Along with Pancake Magisword, it's part of a tasty breakfast.

Waffle Magisword can create the perfect protective shield against a Pancake Magisword assault.

Walk the Plank Magisword

Function: Makes planks.

Fun Fact: Need a plank? Fire up this Magisword and create a bunch of cool ones! Make your friends walk them when they've been naughty.

Warm Hug Magisword

Function: Gives hugs.

Fun Fact: Everyone needs a hug occasionally.

How about a hug, sis?

Of course, brother! But not right now. I'm very busy doing . . . um . . . other things.

Wickersnapper Magisword

Function: Creates wicker objects such as baskets and coverings.

Fun Fact: It can be used to make long wicker vines that are perfect for swinging, whipping, and decorating your home office.

Psst. **Don't tell anyone this but I like to use the ol' Wickersnapper Magisword to tickle Vambre's shoulder when she's not paying attention. One time she thought it was a ghost.**

X-Ray Magisword

Function: X-rays things.

Fun Fact: X-rays can help you see inside yourself.

Zombie Pumpkin Magisword

Function: Shoots Seeds of the Undead that can eat through things.

Fun Fact: Famous moves include the Zombie Bark Buster, Zombie Mush Masher, and Zombie Fungus Fist.

This li'l guy is part zombie, part pumpkin, and all Magisword! He loves chowing down on fresh pumpkin guts. He's like a zombie for that stuff. He also has the unique ability to regenerate body parts that may have been ripped off or eaten.

An enviable ability, to say the least. Just don't call him *punkin*. He hates that.

Hate is a very strong word. I'd say it's not my favorite.

WOW. That was a lot of Magiswords. It all happened so fast! I can barely remember them all now.

I do. I remember them *all* and I shall honor them with every breath I take.

Well, alrighty then. See ya later!